Why Did My Teacher Cry Today?

A Homework Tale

By Renee Lovekids

Halo
PUBLISHING
INTERNATIONAL

ISBN: 978-1-61244-665-3
Library of Congress Control Number: 2018951383

Printed in the United States of America

Published by Halo Publishing International
1100 NW Loop 410
Suite 700 - 176
San Antonio, Texas 78213
1-877-705-9647
www.halopublishing.com
contact@halopublishing.com

To the baby boy Mikey
To the little boy in Mike and Sam
To Eugene Jr. my biggest fan
To my supportive and humorous parents
To inquisitive children everywhere
To parents that dutifully guide
and encourage their children
To Him who makes all things possible

Have you ever seen a teacher cry? Well, unfortunately, my class has. It actually caught us all by surprise. We never saw it coming. This is *Señora Cruz*.[*] She's a popular teacher at my school. Usually, she is really funny, like when she says, "Spread love, not germs!" when someone sneezes or coughs without covering their mouth. She's trained every class she's taught to say that line as a way of helping to protect her students from the enemy of all children, "GERMS"! *Señora Cruz's* class is an adventure for students. She loves showing off the class to visitors. When parents or guests come to our classroom, we stand and sing "The Welcome Song."

---

[*] *Señora Cruz*—Mrs. Cruz

"Welcome, welcome to our class. Glad you are with us. Shake hands, no time to be blue. Welcome to you!" When we sing the part, "Shake hands, no time to be blue," we walk towards our guests and begin to shake their hands. (*Señora Cruz* quickly comes with us to squirt a small amount of sanitizer in the visitors' hands to fight off GERMS!) The guests are really impressed with us and the song. We feel good too, but not as good as *Señora Cruz*.

The thing my teacher loves best of all is giving homework! Sometimes we feel she lives to give *tarea*.[*] As far as *Señora Cruz* is concerned there is never a reason not to give homework. "Homework is a very important part of learning," she says. It helps us to practice what we've learned during the day and reinforce our skills. "It's a time to spend with your parents or big sister or brother to get their help and talk about your day," she adds.

Yes, *Señora Cruz* will sometimes give four homework assignments, five homework assignments, or even six homework assignments in one night! My friend Jenae says she's never encountered a teacher who loves homework as much as our teacher does. Tiffany agrees.

---

[*] *Tarea*—Homework

1. Computer Reading
2. Create a Math 3 digit word problem
3. Social Studies page 45-50
4. Practice song for the play
5. Explain what a caption is

Homework
Hall Of Shame

To make sure our homework is done, she has a chart in the class that says Homework Hall of Shame! Nobody wants their name on that list. It's there for all to see. Our Principal can see it when she visits, but worst of all, our parents can see it when they visit.

As I said, my teacher loves giving *tarea*. Some teachers in my school will not give any homework at all on the weekend, but not my teacher. "There is never a reason to not do homework!" she says. She will only allow students to miss nine homework assignments during the school year. That translates to one homework assignment per month. I remember when Noah and Jason had already missed fifteen homework assignments, and it was only January! Their parents were called. You should have seen them squirm!

That was all Noah and Jason needed to get them back on track with their studies. Their grades improved considerably after the meeting, and they eventually even became honor students. Maybe this is proof of what *Señora Cruz* attempts to convey to us about doing our homework consistently. Maybe it was just a coincidence.

Some teachers give out "No Homework Passes" to their students. Malcolm and Caleb were brave enough to ask if *Señora Cruz* could give homework passes, like Mrs. Gracie and Mrs. Leena do. *Señora Cruz* responded, "Homework is very important and there is never a reason not to give homework." She did, however, give us three homework assignments that day instead of five. Malcolm and Caleb were our heroes for a day. I repeat, for one day.

Yes, *Señora Cruz* certainly loves homework. She takes great pleasure in saying, *"Saquen su tarea!".* *

---

* *Saquen su tarea*—Take out your homework

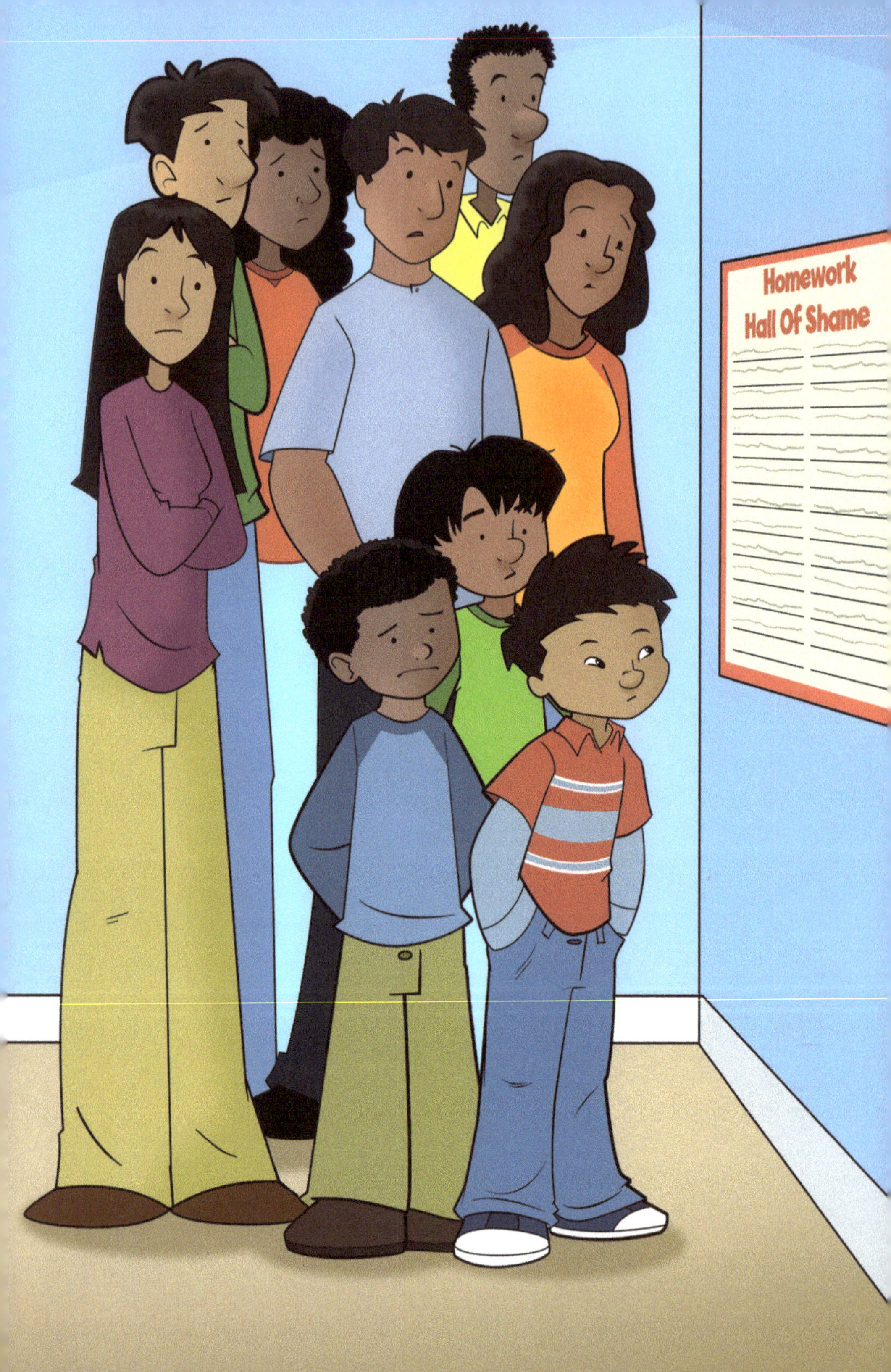
Homework
Hall Of Shame

I will never forget the Parent Teacher Conference last March. My classmate, Aaron, and I were talking out in the hall. We were waiting for *Señora Cruz* to invite our parents into the classroom.

We looked at Michael, Samuel, and Eddie who were getting fidgety as they waited for their parents to be called. They had missed fifteen homework assignments, which was displayed for all to see on the Homework Hall of Shame chart. Their parents were invited in at the same time because the three of them talked a lot in class and played pranks together. The boys came in and tried to block the chart by standing in front of it. "Yeah, nice try, guys," I thought to myself. They know *Señora Cruz* has all that information in her data book. *Señora Cruz* directed Michael, Samuel, and Eddie's parents to the chart.

The parents all screeched and gasped upon seeing it. And then, the fireworks began. There were screams and threats made. Samuel's mother burst into tears. Eddie's mother popped him across the back of his head. Michael's dad started to loosen his belt. *Señora Cruz* looked surprised at their reaction. I think she felt sorry for the boys too, but homework is very important to her and it was her duty to inform their parents for their own good. "Glad I'm not in their shoes," Aaron said. "I wouldn't be allowed to play with the electronic gifts I got during Hanukkah for months!"

J'Lynn, Z'nya, and Tiffany were all smiles that night. They didn't have any checks next to their names on the homework chart. What a night!

To understand *Señora Cruz*, you have to know her story. She loves telling our class stories about herself from when she was a child. Her parents were from the Dominican Republic. She was born in New York. Her parents always encouraged her to read and to study hard. She loved writing and reading. *Señora Cruz* would make up stories about her family and classmates. When it came to doing homework, she looooved it! She was the girl in the class that never missed a homework assignment. It was always neat and she would do extra homework for extra credit. *Señora Cruz* did this without her teachers asking her to! What kid does that?

She remembers running errands with her mother with her homework in tow. She would read her assignments as she rode on the bus with her dad. She would play math games as she shopped with her mother in department stores. In the summer, she would read all the books suggested for Summer Reads and add more to the list! Reading those books kept her busy as her parents and siblings drove to various beaches and amusement parks.

She told us that all her teachers enjoyed having her in their class. She became a homework helper in middle school. Her parents were so proud of her, and they would brag about *Señora Cruz* to their families and friends.

In college, the homework was complicated, but she said that didn't stop her from enjoying it. She tutored in college and got paid for it! She enjoyed volunteering her services as a homework tutor in elementary schools. That was the beginning of her desire to become a teacher.

What *Señora Cruz* doesn't realize is that most kids don't enjoy homework as much as she does. Well, maybe J'Lynn, Z'nya, and Tiffany do. They get good grades and ALWAYS do their homework. They love the stories *Señora Cruz* shares about her childhood. Many of us whisper, "That wouldn't be us making up extra homework," as she speaks of her memorable homework tales. No way! Malcolm says he would watch videos as he rode with his parents for weekend trips. Eddie says he would rather make the excuse that his dog ate the homework than turn in his homework on time every week.

The next day, *Señora Cruz* appeared quite somber. After lunch, she expressed her sentiments about the events that had taken place during the Parent Teacher Conference.

She was concerned by the reaction of Michael, Samuel, and Eddie's parents on the homework issue. So, she decided to engage the class in an activity that would allow us to express our thoughts on the subject of **Homework**. She asked which debate format we would prefer. Would it be the **Ball-Toss Debate** or the **Four Corners Debate**? We really had to think about our options because both debates are fun and entertaining. The **Ball-Toss Debate** is interesting because we choose if we are for or against a topic. Next, we go to the area of our positions, and then we are allowed to move our desk around and actually face our classmates who have the opposing view!

We pass a ball around and you can only speak if you are holding the ball! Bryce and Jaden lost their temper during one debate and Jaden threw the ball at Bryce! That topic of debate was "Which is the better sport: baseball or basketball?" Jaden is in a baseball league, and Bryce. . . you guessed it, he's in a basketball league. *Señora Cruz* was not happy about that incident at all, and they were given additional homework to write in favor of the opposite view and to add why that sport is so popular.

Our class chose the **Four Corner Debate** because it allowed us to get out of our seats and move around during the debate, but it's not so "in your face" as the **Ball-Toss Debate**. The positions are posted within the four corners of our classroom. The positions are: **Agree, Disagree, Strongly Agree,** and **Strongly Disagree**. These positions can also be changed to fit the topic. One example might be the topic of making mistakes. The positions could be: **Scared, Embarrassed, I Don't Care,** or **Shy**.

We headed for our corners to discuss our stances and to decide who would take notes and who would speak for us within our groups. We walked to our corners and to my amazement, students actually joined the **Strongly Agree** and **Agree** corners. I shouldn't have been surprised to see J'lynn, Z'nya, Tiffany, Rosa, and José in those groups. Weirdos!

Señora Cruz allotted ten minutes for the preparation and set her timer. The **strongly agree** group believed that homework helps them to perform better in class and on tests, and they displayed their test as evidence. The **agree** group believed homework is necessary, but that it should be more interesting, such as recognizing the **main idea** of a movie or popular kids' show, instead of a boring passage. They also argued for no homework on Fridays. The **disagree** group believed that homework shouldn't be assigned on Fridays, and they preferred a weekly quiz in various subjects instead. Lastly, the **strongly disagree** group argued that homework should never be given on Fridays. They felt homework should only be assigned two or three times a week as projects when possible.

Needless to say, it was an interesting debate and *Señora Cruz* listened intently. We didn't totally change her mind during the debate, but we were only responsible for three homework assignments that day, and our class considered that a win!

I have to admit; we have a knowledgeable and intelligent class. We are well behaved too, well... most of the time. Our Principal had begun a Best Behavior campaign. The class who won the most Best Behavior certificates for the month has two options to choose from. We came in second place once and had an ice cream party. We had a great time, and *Señora Cruz* was so proud of us.

As I mentioned earlier, *Señora Cruz* enjoys showing off her class. She wanted us to win first place! Well, we were quiet in the halls, and teachers made recommendations for our class and awarded us those certificates. We behaved in the staircase and during recess. We received so many compliments. I must confess that as hard as it sometimes was to be on our best behavior, getting recognized felt good!

One day during second period, an announcement was made over the intercom: "P.S. 912 is proud to announce that *Señora Cruz's* class 4-313 has won first place in the Best Behavior contest. Congratulations!" The voice spoke with enthusiasm. Our class burst into shouts of excitement. You could hear us celebrating even from down the hallway. Then Mrs. Aneeta came to our class to inquire what our choice would be. *Señora Cruz* quickly said, "We'll have the pizza party!"

A few of our classmates rallied behind her and shouted "Yes, a pizza party! We're gonna have a pizza *fiesta*!"* Mrs. Aneeta noticed we were not all that enthused. There was still the other option. She asked us if we wanted that option. The majority of the class said, "Yes!" *Señora Cruz* looked puzzled and said, "You would prefer the other option over the pizza party? We can eat, do salsa dancing, and have a karaoke contest! I'll bring the punch and fruit juice," she added. Her supporters agreed. The rest of the class remained quiet. *Señora Cruz's* puzzled look became a disappointed glare. When Mrs. Aneeta announced we could have the second option, we exploded with applause and laughter. That's when it happened. Our teacher went to her desk and began to cry. At first it was just a whimper. We couldn't believe it. Actually, it was quite sad.

---

* *Fiesta*—Party

She was really upset that as a class we had chosen the second option. I guess you are wondering what the other option was. It was something that interrupted what *Señora Cruz* loves to do.

Another broadcast was made over the intercom to announce the prize. The voice declared: "*Señora Cruz's* class 4-313 will get a three-day No Homework Pass! Congratulations!" Mrs. Aneeta and Principal Thea came to the class with the passes. Thunderous shouts erupted in our classroom from the students and *Señora Cruz*, well. . .

Author's Notes

Homework has been the subject of controversy for decades. The opinions are vast and the arguments around it are heated!

It's a great topic to introduce to primary learners between the ages of 7-11. It becomes more interesting for junior high and high school learners who have considerably greater vocabulary skills than elementary children, along with critical thinking skills and verbal/oral competencies.

Using **debates** to express a learner's point of view is a medium that teaches students to listen as well as speak. It's also a tool to develop **critical thinking** skills, develop and use academic vocabulary capabilities for expression, and practice oral skills.

This book targets primary learners. I am well aware of the pressure on these students to perform well on assessments and to conform to **Common Core Standards**. **College Readiness** is the buzzword and rigor its companion. Exposing elementary school age learners to the art of **debates** will give them the advantage of starting early to develop reasoning and analytical skills methodically. What I mean by methodically is that the skills are taught in a way that is intentional, organized, and orderly. Instruction for these practices should be given gradually, at the learners' pace.

Debate Formats Mentioned in the Story

Four-Corner Debates: A non-threatening activity that allows students to discuss controversial topics. Students are able to move around the classroom while using their critical thinking skills. Students are given a topic and asked to choose sides. Next, they prepare their arguments for ten minutes. They decide who will write and who will be the speaker. Then, they go to the sign that matches the position they have chosen. Their options are: Agree, Disagree, Strongly Agree, and Strongly Disagree. The debate begins. If a student changes their position, they can physically move to the corresponding area.

Ball-Toss Debate: This debate format is one that allows for mobility as well. Students are given a topic, and they must take a side. They situate themselves according to whether they are for or against the topic. The interesting factor here is the students arrange the desks so that each side is facing the opposition (a bit confrontational). Students sit on their desks and take turns tossing a ball to discuss their position on the topic. You have to have the ball in your hand in order to speak.

Other Formats to Consider

- Fishbowl Debates
- Role Play Debate
- Inner Circle, Outer Circle Debate Strategy
- Stage a Debate

www.ingramcontent.com/pod-product-compliance
Lightning Source LLC
Chambersburg PA
CBHW041922090426
42741CB00019B/3451